Search and Learn

by Leslie Mills
illustrated by John Martin

Practice Decodable 43

Mc Graw Hill Education

Bothell, WA • Chicago, IL • Columbus, OH • New York, NY

MHEonline.com

Send all inquiries to:
McGraw-Hill Education
8787 Orion Place
Columbus, OH 43240

ISBN: 978-0-02-145551-5
MHID: 0-02-145551-1

Printed in China

8 9 10 11 12 DSS 27 26 25 24 23

Pearl searched the dirt.
Kids heard a tap, tap, tap.

Earl and Dad met Pearl.

Earl asked, "Are any objects in the earth?"

"Objects from the past are stuck in the earth," said Pearl.

Pearl added, “I like to learn from the objects.”

"A man from the past earned cash with this," said Pearl.

"First, I will have a glass of water. Then I will search the earth more."